RISE FROM THE ABYSS

Arenzungla Jamir

Presentation by *BookLeaf Publishing*

Web: www.bookleafpub.com

E-mail: info@bookleafpub.com

ISBN: 9789395621366

First edition 2022

DEDICATION

To all survivors of injustice,

and to the people who give hope.

ACKNOWLEDGEMENT

My publishers and I would like to deeply acknowledge Limatola Longkumer for permission to copyright material for the book cover - the Coral Heart, from her collection of art illustrations.

THEY SAY

They say she cannot play,
too slow, an old grandmother can slay;
but she plays Archimedes calculus,
behind she does not stay.

They say she is not pure,
does not deserve Adam for sure.
As they pronounce from the Chief Justice chair,
she fought to present her ill heart a cure.

They say she will not make it to Philly,
she is trying to make herself look silly.
It does not occur to their ant brains;
she is just trying to make a difference really.

They say she is not cut out for limelight,
too bad, she is not Dorothy Day bright.
Though they open their whale mouth,
she has a heart to share the light.

Shakespeare's Romance

He smiled. She smiled
He knew. She knew.
Together they cannot be,
but loved like Shakespeare's romance.
Holding her,
He said, "All we can do is love each other".

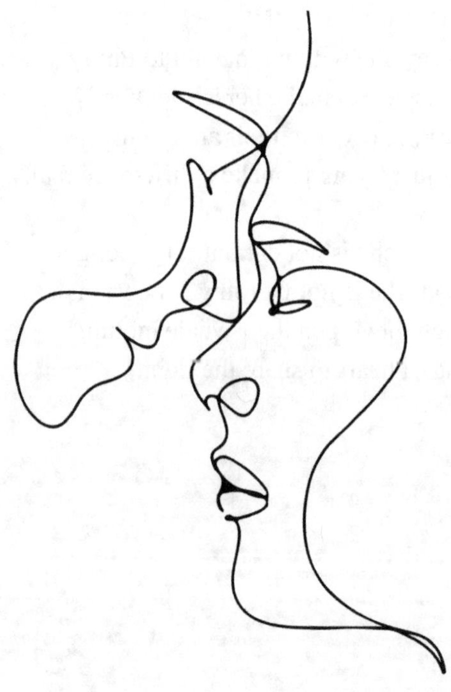

THE DROP

If a man can spread her,
go deep and drop a seed
making a special being;
How hard can it be
for a man to spread her wings,
go deep into her soul and drop a word
to create a powerful her.

A MOTHER'S LOVE

A love that is so pure,
filled with passion and care;
That blossoms day by day.
Where can we find?

A love that covers with protection,
as under eagle's wings;
Pulling close to a kind heart.
Where can we find?

A love that never leaves,
even in times of trouble and sickness.
Always keeping in prayers.
Where can we find?

The love that we ask,
which is endless and special.
Drawing strength from High,
can be found in a Mother's love.

PAIN

Pain is loving
and losing,
and knowing,
and realizing
and accepting,
that life is unfair.

TALKING EYEBROWS

Girl, you need not say much
Why waste precious energy?
That alluring voice needs saving,
for a great many things.
Instead, do the talk
with those mighty eyebrows
and walk away like a Queen.

WHISPERS IN THE WIND

The wind blows past the madding crowd
and all the people could only hear,
"susurrus! susurrus! susurrus!"
But she hears-
"You are love"
"You are a goddess"
"You are worth it"
She keeps walking, smiling, thanking
and lost in the wind.
She get the confused, flabbergasted,
and startling looks
As though she is possessed,
When actually she is enlightened.

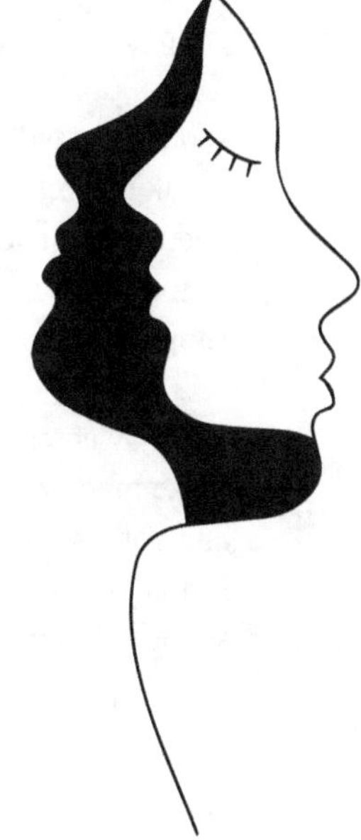

YOU WERE SUPPOSED TO PROTECT ME

I, only wanted to run around in circles,
admiring my pretty summer dress
and not play horsey.
I thought you would be the cool uncle,
supposed to protect me.

I, only wanted to do my homework,
get good grades, top the class
and not be left in utter shock.
I thought you would give me a father's love,
supposed to protect me.

I, only wanted to report,
speak up, get justice
and not be handled wrong.
I thought you respect your uniform,
supposed to protect me.

I, only wanted to know you,
make memories in love
and not leave me in bewilderment.
I thought you would be the guy,
supposed to protect me.

I, only wanted a partner,
build a home, get support
and not have dark spots on my body.
I thought you would be a loving man,
supposed to protect me.

I, only wanted to learn,
be guided, educated
and not be treated ugly.
I thought you would be a great teacher,
supposed to protect me.

I, only wanted to take the short route,
get home, rest for the day
and not crawl in a bleeding state.
I thought you all were gentlemen,
supposed to protect me.

I, now know,
you claiming to protect,
is all a lie.
I, summon the warrior in me,
armoured to the core.
And I will win.

SHOES THAT CREATE MAGIC

Remember, those feet are meant to walk away,
from agony, scorn or half-hearted love.

Then, pick up that tall pair,
wear them like you own your life,
sway your hips from side to side,
and don't look back.

IN A PARALLEL WORLD

When their eyes meet,
they feel a deep love;
strong as death.
Wanting, craving,
needing to give,
burning like blazing fire,
as they brush against each other by chance.
Restricted by a boundary,
they say, "In a parallel world, we will be each
other's".

NIGHTSHADE

Too many have suffered,
tolerated,
abused,
ill-treated,
wronged,
manipulated.
So why ask,
"Why adorn with Nightshade instead of dainty
daisies?"
When you should know,
the kind of purpose it can have.
As it did for Livia Drusilla and Antigone,
to defend and escape.

REGRET

Regret is the dark beast,
you feel you can't defeat,
towering you,
as if picking at your brain.

Breathe in. Breathe out.

Forgive yourself.

Move on.

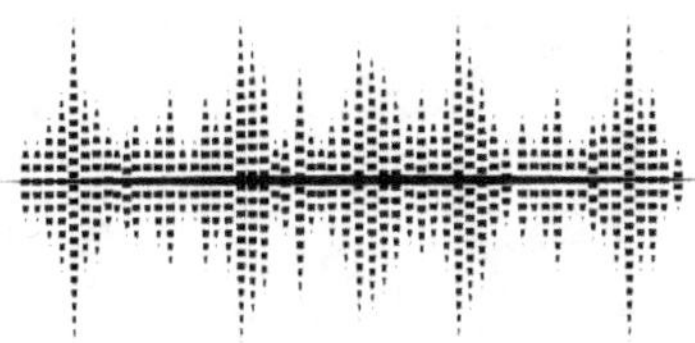

BALANCE

Maybe the three beautiful words aren't enough,
to love and be loved.
As the saying goes -
Actions speak louder than words.

Maybe we do not need guns and violence,
to save and be saved.
We only need to learn,
that words can also win battles.

It's all about **the BALANCE.**

WHAT HAPPENS AT ROOFTOPS?

Sometimes as daunting as it can be,
to take the flight of stairs,
but you reach atop the building anyway.
Sitting at the edge with legs dangling in the air,
you look down and wonder
if you would perish or survive the fall.
Still looking down,
you think the latter would be tragic.
You hear faint voices from across another
building;
looking up,
you see humans drinking, laughing and dancing.
Staring at them,
you find it meaningless.
In another dim lit rooftop,
twining with the party building,
you see two figures caressing under the moon.
Your lips curl into a smile for a while.
Then,
You look to your right,
and you see the crescent moon.
Then, to your left,
and you see the cross.
You let out a sigh,

and look down again.
A voice deep within,
reminds you to look up,
and admire the stars for one last time.
And you think to yourself,
how wonderful it is to do
what you love to do.
Just then, you realize how stars are formed,
squeezed under enough pressure,
within the clouds of dust,
collapsing under its own gravitational attraction.

You let out,
painful,
joyful,
ugly,
crocodile tears.
You pull yourself up,
shake it off,
turn around from the edge,
knowing that,
a star is born.

HERE AND NOW

You may be here,
by love,
by mistake,
by coincidence,
by force,
by arrangement.
Whatever it may look like,
you needed to be here,
because you matter.
You are here to learn,
unlearn,
share your story,
in all its glory.
Here and now.

JUNGRARA

Whenever you feel lost,
and lonely,
and unloved;
Remember,
you are "Jungrara".
Take in this Ao- Naga word,
and know that it means
something beyond good,
beautiful,
magnificent,
a beautiful creation,
which is YOU.

THE SHAPESHIFTER
WOMAN

Woman,
you are more than the labels
this world put on you.
A majestic shapeshifter you are,
possessing a wild force and energy,
that allows people to accept who they are,
because you embrace your inner-strength
and not be defined by worldly jabber.

A-BUN-DANCE

When you are beaten and bruised
And slouching from the pain,
and feeling drenched as if in heavy rain,
Do not ever think you are cursed.

Though your world may feel shaken
And sitting at the edge of the bed,
carrying a face that looks more than sad,
Never give up the hope to awaken.

And when you feel short of grace,
Forget not the many miraculous saving,
and the showers of unmerited giving,
For you are invited to do A-BUN-DANCE